THE LIBRARY OF
AMERICAN
LIVES AND TIMES™

# JIM BOWIE

## Frontier Legend, Alamo Hero

J. R. Edmondson

The Rosen Publishing Group's
PowerPlus Books™
New York

*To Patty Miller and Linda Gardner,*
*and to the Daughters of the Republic of Texas,*
*all of whom keep the spirit of James Bowie alive*

Published in 2003 by The Rosen Publishing Group, Inc.
29 East 21st Street, New York, NY 10010

First Edition

*Editor's Note: All quotations have been reproduced as they appeared in*
*the letters and diaries from which they were borrowed. No correction was*
*made to the inconsistent spelling that was common in that time period.*

### Library of Congress Cataloging-in-Publication Data

Edmondson, J. R., 1950–
Jim Bowie : hero of the Alamo / J. R. Edmondson.
    p. cm. — (Library of American lives and times)
Includes bibliographical references and index.
Summary: Describes the tumultuous times in early Texas history that
formed the character of Jim Bowie, who is known both for inventing
the Bowie knife and for fighting and dying at the Alamo.
  ISBN 0-8239-5734-9 (library binding)
1. Bowie, James, d. 1836—Juvenile literature. 2. Pioneers—Texas—
Biography—Juvenile literature. 3. Alamo (San Antonio,
Tex.)—Siege, 1836—Juvenile literature. 4. Texas—History—To 1846—
Juvenile literature. [1. Bowie, James, d. 1836. 2. Pioneers. 3. Alamo
(San Antonio, Tex.)—Siege, 1836. 4. Texas—History—To 1846.] I. Title.
II. Series.
  F389.B8 E36 2003
  976.4'03'092—dc21

2001004954

Manufactured in the United States of America

# CONTENTS

# Introduction

"By Hercules! The man was greater than Caesar or Cromwell—nay, nearly equal to Odin or Thor! The Texans ought to build him an altar!"

A Texas newspaper, the *Telegraph and Texas Register* (June 20, 1850) attributed the above exclamation to the Scottish historian and biographer Thomas Carlyle. According to the newspaper account, a visiting American minister, Theodore Parker, had just related to Carlyle the exploits of James Bowie.

However, in a sense there were two Bowies, the James Bowie of history, and the "Big Jim" Bowie who crossed into legend. Which Bowie did Parker describe to Carlyle to generate such enthusiasm?

James Bowie left a very limited amount of historical documentation. He did not keep a diary, record his memoirs, or even write many letters. He never wrote a single word about his knife, nor did he ever relate his version of

In 2001, the state of Texas bought the only known painting of James Bowie made during his life, from the estate of one of Bowie's descendants. The painting is generally attributed to American painter George Peter Alexander Healy and is thought to have been made in the 1830s.

the Sandbar Fight, the violent dispute that made both him and his knife famous. He provided only a very brief report about his desperate battle with the Indians near the San Saba River, which was fought while he was seeking lost silver mines. If he wrote any letters from the Alamo, they have not survived. We must rely instead on the accounts of others, like his brothers Rezin and John, and his friend Caiaphas Ham, who either witnessed the events or heard about them directly from Jim.

These events alone were enough to make Bowie a hero of his time. Yet in the absence of documentation, after Bowie's death these events and others became further exaggerated and embellished. Bowie emerged as a knight errant, wielding an American version of King Arthur's sword, Excalibur. More than a dozen men claimed, or were credited with, the invention of the Bowie knife. Newspapers of the late nineteenth century reported that Bowie had engaged in numerous deadly knife fights, usually while rescuing the weak from evil. However, no historical evidence exists to support any of these violent encounters.

The popular image of Big Jim Bowie continued into the middle of the twentieth century. He was featured in novels, movies, and even a television series.

However, there was a dark side to James Bowie, and it, too, was beginning to emerge. He had been a slave smuggler and a land swindler. It hardly mattered that many of his contemporaries had engaged in these same practices, which, in that day, were not considered all that immoral. People looking back on his actions today, recognized the terrible evil of slavery, and believed Bowie was a bad man. In 1988, the National Association for the Advancement of Colored People (NAACP) campaigned against naming a new Austin, Texas, high school for James Bowie. In 1999, there was a similar movement to rename the Bowie Elementary School in Dallas.

The historical James Bowie was a complex figure. He was a rogue, and not always in the most romantic sense of the word. Yet he was loyal, he was fearless, and he became a hero in every sense of the word. The state of Texas seems finally to have reconciled the bad parts of his character with the good and has embraced him again. In June 2001, the state paid $322,000 to acquire the only known portrait of James Bowie painted during his lifetime. This is the true story of the historical James Bowie.

# 1. The Louisiana Territory

On March 6, 1836, while Texas was trying to win its independence from Mexico, James Bowie, along with David Crockett, William Barret Travis, and some two hundred other Texans, called Texians in Bowie's time, died defending the old Alamo mission-fortress against about two thousand Mexican soldiers, or *soldados*. Bowie's death transformed him into a martyr and ensured his ranking among the most famous of all of Texas's heroes. Even before the Alamo, Big Jim Bowie's legendary knife had already carved his name into the pages of history.

In a sense Bowie inherited the struggle for liberty. His ancestors had fought for Scotland's freedom from England. The Bowie clan had occupied Stirlingshire, on the edge of the Scottish highlands. At Stirling Bridge, William Wallace had defeated English forces in 1297. Seventeen years later, at nearby Bannockburn, Robert the Bruce had finally won Scottish independence. Perhaps the participation of Bowie warriors in those battles led to the origin of the Bowie clan motto: *Quod Non Pro Patria*, or What Not For Country.

Sir William Wallace wanted Scotland to be independent of English rule.
Though he defeated the English at Stirling Bridge, he was defeated by
Edward I of England in 1298. In 1305, Wallace was captured and
brought to London, where he was hanged, drawn, and quartered. This
statue of Wallace, located in Aberdeen, was created around 1930.

The motto accompanies the traditional Bowie coat of arms, which depicts a shield bearing a diagonal band with three buckles. A lion rises behind the shield, holding aloft a dagger, or dirk. In spirit, if not in design, the Bowie knife descended from the fearsome Scottish dirk.

The ancient roots of the Bowie family tree included Bue the Thick, a Viking warrior, and Eocha Bui, who became King Eugene IV and reigned over Scotland from 605 to 621.

In 1581, the Scottish king, James VI, awarded a house and a garden in Cowper to "Jerome Bowie, Master of the King's Wines." In appreciation, Jerome christened his son James. It became traditional for almost every subsequent Bowie generation to name a son in honor of James VI.

Other honorable Bowie ancestors served as burgesses, constables, and magistrates. However, there also were outlaws in the Bowie clan. In 1602, John Bowie led a raid on lands owned by the sheriff of Moray. Eight years later authorities arrested William Bowie for "striking his dirk into Alaster Reach." The sap that flowed through the Bowie family tree contained the blood of both heroes and scoundrels.

In 1742, James Bowie, who one day would be the grandfather of Big Jim Bowie, sailed to Maryland in the British colonies of North America. He married Sarah Whitehead, and the couple eventually settled in the Georgia colony.

They christened their first son Rezin, after Sarah's father. As young Rezin matured, his signature on documents reveals that he generally preferred the phonetic spelling of his name, "Reason."

At that time North America was divided among European nations. The Spanish explorers and conquistadors who followed Columbus had established the first and largest European empire in North America. Centered at Mexico City, which had risen over the conquered Aztec capital, Tenochtitlan, New Spain encompassed most of South America, all of central America, the southwestern portion of North America, and the region called Florida.

Great Britain occupied the Atlantic seaboard north of Florida and westward to the Appalachian Mountains. The area was divided into thirteen separate British colonies.

Before the French and Indian War (1754–1763), France claimed Canada and the vast Louisiana Territory that extended westward from the Appalachians to the Rocky Mountains. France's claim to the area that included Texas conflicted with Spain's claim to Texas.

When France lost the French and Indian War, it gave up, or forfeited, all of its North American empire. Britain acquired Canada and the part of Louisiana east of the Mississippi River. Spain received the Louisiana Territory west of the Mississippi.

English colonists were anxious to migrate across the Appalachians into the newly acquired British frontier

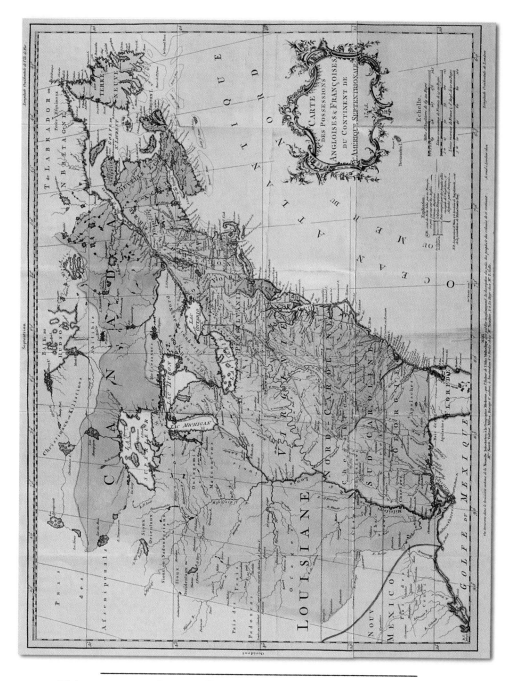

This 1755 French map illustrates the French and British colonial interests in North America. The original thirteen British colonies are colored yellow. The Louisiana Territory is in green. During the French and Indian War, the two nations fought over the area, here colored red, between the Mississippi River and the Appalachian Mountains.

that at that time extended to the Mississippi. Many of the Native American peoples that occupied the region had been allies of the defeated, French, and they remained hostile to English settlers. To protect his American subjects, King George III issued an order restricting them from traveling into the wilderness beyond the Appalachians. The colonists resented this ban. When the king also tried to impose several taxes to help pay off debts from the war, the colonists grew increasingly angry. In 1776, the situation finally boiled over with the Battle of Lexington and Concord. The American Revolution had begun.

When the thirteen colonies rebelled against Great Britain, young Reason became yet another Bowie who fought for independence. In October 1779, he participated in the American attempt to recapture Savannah, Georgia, from the British. The battle, the bloodiest since Bunker Hill, proved a disaster for the Americans. Reason was among the eight hundred dead or wounded in the defeated Colonial army. Elve Ap-Catesby Jones, the daughter of a Welsh immigrant, helped care for his injuries. Reason fell in love with his nurse.

On October 19, 1781, the British army surrendered at Yorktown, Virginia, effectively ending the war. The American colonial leaders created modern history's first great experiment in self-government. The thirteen colonies became the United States of America.

Reason and Elve married on March 8, 1782. Their union eventually would produce at least ten children, two of whom would die in infancy.

Suddenly there were no more barriers across the Appalachians. A flood of pioneers pushed westward into the forested wilderness, opening new territories and creating new states to be added to the infant nation.

Reason and Elve Bowie eagerly joined the migration. Reason possessed the true pioneer spirit, always seeking to carve a new home, a new beginning, out of the wilderness. His son, John Jones Bowie, who had been born in 1785 before the family left Georgia, recalled:

> *My father was passionately fond of the adventures and excitements of a woodsman's life, and as the country improved and opened, population increased, and the refinements of civilization encroached upon the freedom of his hunting-grounds, he retired to wilder regions, where he could enjoy those sports and stirring adventures peculiar to a frontier life.*

The Bowies briefly settled in Sumner County, in the north-central part of what would soon become Tennessee. On September 8, 1793, Elve delivered a son named Rezin Pleasant Bowie.

Early the next year, Reason moved his growing family north across the border into what was then Logan County, in the newly created state of Kentucky. He built

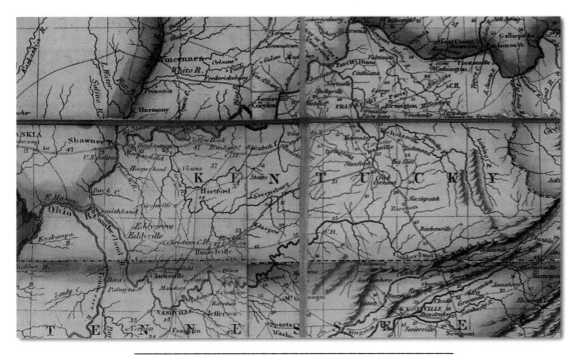

The Bowies moved to Kentucky just one year after it earned its statehood. Eastern Kentucky is mountainous and wild. To the west the landscape becomes flat, and the soil is ideal for farming. This map, created around 1816, was compiled by John Melish and engraved by John Vallance and Henry Schenck Tanner.

a house and a gristmill on 200 acres (81 ha) watered by Terrapin Creek. His most famous son was born there in the spring of 1796. Reason and Elve named the boy James, continuing the tradition of honoring King James VI of Scotland. The boy was sometimes called by the nickname Jim.

A year or so later, a younger brother named Stephen joined the family. Then Reason Bowie decided again that it was time to move to wilder regions. He was running out of U.S. territory to which he could move. The Mississippi River hugged the western tip of Kentucky.

James Bowie's birthplace and birthdate are the first of many mysteries surrounding the Alamo's history. Five states (Maryland, Georgia, Tennessee, Kentucky, and Louisiana) have claimed to be the birthplace of James Bowie.

Perhaps it should not have been a controversy. In 1852, John Jones Bowie, older brother of James, wrote that their father, Rezin, "removed to Logan County, Kentucky, where my brother James was born in the spring of 1796." Of the many who have written about Bowie's birthplace, John was the only one who was actually there at the time.

In 1989, historian Joseph Musso, aided by researchers and archivists in Tennessee and Kentucky, finally uncovered property deeds that substantiated John Jones Bowie's statement. However, no historical evidence has surfaced that provides James Bowie's actual date of birth. For now, perhaps forever, his birthdate must remain a mystery.

Beyond that lay the Spanish portion of the Louisiana Territory called Missouri.

A few American pioneers already had secured permission from Spain to settle in Missouri. The first had been a Connecticut Yankee named Moses Austin, who came to Missouri seeking lead mines. In 1798, Austin established the first Anglo American settlement west of the Mississippi at present-day Potosi, Missouri.

The next year the most famous of all American pioneers, Daniel Boone, then sixty-five years old, drifted from Kentucky into the Missouri bootheel. "Too many people! Too crowded! I want more elbow room," Boone said to explain his move. Reason Bowie might have given the same explanation for his own move to Missouri. In 1800, he settled near New Madrid. The possibility exists that a very young James Bowie might have met his neighbor, the legendary Daniel Boone. However James Bowie's destiny would be more closely connected with the son of Moses Austin. Three years older than James, Stephen Fuller Austin would one day be known as the Father of Texas.

The same year that Reason Bowie moved into Missouri, Spain returned the Louisiana Territory to France. Three years later, in 1803, the United States purchased Louisiana, virtually doubling the size of the young nation.

By then Reason Bowie had decided to move again. He secured a flatboat and floated his family down the

Mississippi River, landing within the borders of the modern state of Louisiana. They moved around, finally settling near Opelousas, St. Landry Parish, in the central part of the state. There, about 1810, Reason Bowie acquired a large tract of land and established a modest plantation where he owned some twenty slaves. He would spend his final years on that plantation, raising cotton and sawing lumber.

James Bowie was then in his midteens. He and his brother, Rezin Pleasant, had inherited their father's love for the wilderness. Avid hunters, they became keen marksmen with their long rifles. However, they preferred a more sporting method of stalking big game. They galloped through the forests, roping deer and wild cattle, and then killing the lassoed prey with hunting knives.

John J. Bowie recalled that his younger brother James sometimes roped wild mustangs and rode them for the entertainment of his friends and neighbors. "He has even been known to rope and ride alligators," John Bowie reported.

John also bragged about James's "entirely original" method of capturing bears. The large, aggressive animals were dangerous prey for a lone hunter with a single-shot flintlock rifle. If the rifle ball did not kill a bear instantly, the wounded bear often would charge the hunter before there was time to reload. Even James Bowie preferred not to face a pain-mad bear armed with just a hunting knife.

According to John, James would hammer iron spikes

at an inward angle into a short, hollow log and then put honey inside as bait. John remembered:

> In his eagerness to get the honey, Bruin would thrust his muzzle and head down among the spikes; and when he would attempt to draw his head out, the spikes would pierce the skin and flesh in such a manner as to prevent him from throwing off the mask, and in this blind-folded condition he became an easy prey to his gleeful captors.

James Bowie's mother, Elve, also influenced James and his brothers. She was a remarkable woman, tough enough to endure the frontier existence. She also taught herself to read and write, and then passed on that knowledge to her sons.

The Bowie boys also learned enough math to keep track of their money. At times they were wealthy, at times they were broke. The Bowie brothers were gamblers by nature. They did not restrict their wagers, or bets, to the gaming tables in the local taverns. All of life was their game. They would bet their fortunes, and sometimes their lives, on schemes, enterprises, and adventures.

# 2. Texas

The Bowie family settled onto their plantation in St. Landry Parish, Louisiana. At the same time, Mexico, to the west and south, was following the United States's lead and thinking of independence. In 1810, Father Miguel Hidalgo y Costilla initiated the Mexican Revolution from Spain.

Spanish troops eventually captured and executed Father Hidalgo. However, his revolution refused to die with him. One of Father Hidalgo's loyal followers, Bernardo Gutiérrez, thought of a bold plan. He would recruit an army from the neighboring United States to aid the revolutionaries in northern Mexico. This army would drive the Spanish soldados from the Mexican province of Texas. Texas then would be declared a republic, a nation independent from Spain. In that capacity it would serve both as an example for the rest of Mexico and as a base of operations to press the revolution southward.

Gutiérrez believed this would be an easy task if men from the United States would help. A meager population of only about three thousand Tejanos occupied

Father Miguel Hidalgo, pictured in an 1828 hand-colored lithograph by Claudio Linati, first aroused the suspicions of Spanish authorities when he taught his hungry parishioners new farming methods. Hidalgo later led the villagers in revolt, but was defeated in 1817. The Spaniards caught him, stripped him of his religious robes, and executed him.

*In 1690,
Father Damien Massenet
established the first Spanish mission
among the Hasinai Indians. The priest
mistook their traditional greeting,
"Tayshas" (which translated as "Welcome,
Friend"), for the name of their tribe. Thus
Father Massenet wrongly described their
domain as the "great kingdom
of the Texas." The
name stuck.*

the province, and many of them supported the revolution. Moreover, there only were three towns in Texas: Nacogdoches, La Bahía, or Goliad, and San Antonio de Bexar.

At the time of the revolution, a large Spanish force defended Bexar. Much smaller Spanish garrisons were stationed at Nacogdoches and La Bahía.

In 1812, Bernardo Gutiérrez recruited his revolutionary army in Louisiana. Colonel Augustus Magee left the U.S. Army to serve as co-commander. Together they raised a force of 130 men for their Republican Army of the North.

# A MAP
## of
### THE INTERNAL PROVINCES
## OF
### NEW SPAIN.

*The Outlines are from the Sketches of, but corrected and improved by Captain ZEBULON M. PIKE, who was conducted through that COUNTRY, in the Year 1807, by Order of the Commandant General of those Provinces.*

### REFERENCES.

————— Boundaries between the Provinces
⊛ Capitals of Provinces or Kingdoms
▲ Spanish Villages
▲ Indian Villages or Towns
❧ Spanish Towns of consequence

♜ Fortified Towns or Forts garrisoned
○ Springs or Fountains
◔ Old Towns evacuated
————— Roads
————— Route travelled by the American Troops in 1807.

Country explored by a Detachment of American Troops commanded by Captain PIKE

Sierra de Almagra

Rio de la Plata

Immense Plains used as Pasturage by the Cibolas

Rio Colorado de Natchitoches

Ietan Country

S. Fort de Janaphaye

Indiens Tawaws

Sierra de el Sacramento

Immense Herds of wild Horses

Sierra de Guadalupe

Immense Herds of wild Horses

Philip Nolan killed, and his Party consisting of 11 Americans and 9 Spaniards and French made Prisoners by a Party of Spaniards, several of whom remain Prisoners in the Provinces in 1807.

PROVINCE OF TEXAS

S. Saba

Sabine River

Grand Copper Mines

North

Mexico

Apaches Faraone

PASSO

Rio del Norte

Bolson de Mapimi

Rio del Norte

S. Antonio

Rio Guadalupe

CHIHUAHUA

Sierra de

Province of New Santander

Viceroyalty of Mexico

Monteloyen

Monterey

Administration of Durango

Senaloa

Durango

Gulf of Mexico

Boundary between the Vice Royalty

Division of Maps
MAY 4 1931
Library of Congress

James Bowie was only sixteen years old at the time and did not enlist. Bowie family tradition relates that his nineteen-year-old brother, Rezin, joined the Republican Army of the North. If so, he would have been the first Bowie to fight for Texas liberty.

Marching under a green flag, the small army crossed the Sabine River into Texas in August 1812. Nacogdoches surrendered a few days later. In November the Republicans captured Goliad and camped there for the winter.

During the following spring, the Republican Army of the North grew dramatically in size. Its ranks were swelled by revolutionary Tejanos and by Spanish soldados who sympathized with the cause of independence. Their defections simultaneously reduced the size of the Spanish garrison at San Antonio de Bexar. When the Republican Army arrived outside Bexar on April 1, 1813, the outnumbered Spanish forces surrendered the town.

The revolution had triumphed. The province of Texas had been liberated from Spain and was declared a republic.

Then everything went wrong. A Tejano officer, possibly acting under orders from Gutiérrez, arranged the brutal murders of the Spanish leaders. Disgusted, many of the

---

*Previous page*: In the early 1800s, three towns dotted the vast Texas landscape: Nacogdoches, Goliad, and San Antonio de Bexar. In this map of New Spain, Nacogdoches is outlined in blue and San Antonio de Bexar (called San Antonio here) is outlined in red. The outlines are from the sketches of Zebulon M. Pike, who explored the area in 1807.

Anglo Americans returned to Louisiana. If Rezin Bowie did serve in the Republican Army, he also returned home with them. It may have saved his life.

Already General Joaquín de Arredondo was leading a massive army north to recapture Texas. On August 18, 1813, the Spanish force engaged what was left of the Republican Army near the Medina River south of San Antonio de Bexar. The Republicans were routed, with more than six hundred killed on the battlefield. The first Republic of Texas died with them. It had lasted for only five and a half months.

Those Republicans who escaped the slaughter fled toward the safety of Louisiana. Bexareno families who had sympathized with the Republicans abandoned their homes and joined in the frantic flight to the U.S. borders.

Not everyone made it to Louisiana. General Arredondo's pursuing troops captured several hundred Republicans and Tejano rebels. Arredondo ordered the execution of most of the male prisoners and had their wives and children put in jail.

A nineteen-year-old Spanish lieutenant who had distinguished himself in the battle of the Medina carefully observed Arredondo's ruthless treatment of his prisoners. His name was Antonio López de Santa Anna. He would display even more ruthlessness, twenty-three years later, when he returned to San Antonio at the head of his own army.

In January 1815, General Sir Edward Packenham led the British attack on the Americans in the Battle of New Orleans. The scene shown in this 1817 hand-colored engraving by Joseph Yeager, entitled *Battle of New Orleans and the Death of Major General Packenham on the 8th of January 1815*. The sides met at Chalmette Plantation, a narrow strip of land in the bayous of the Mississippi River delta.

Even as the Spanish forces regained Texas, the United States again fought Great Britain in the War of 1812. The war escalated in September 1814, when British troops captured and burned Washington City, as the nation's capital was then known. Only two months later, a British naval invasion force threatened New Orleans. The war had reached Louisiana.

General Andrew Jackson raised the call for volunteers as he marched to the defense of New Orleans. James Bowie, then eighteen years old, enlisted in the Louisiana

General Andrew Jackson, nicknamed Old Hickory, led 4,000 untrained American frontiersmen and militiamen against more than 8,000 experienced British soldiers in the Battle of New Orleans. He is pictured here in a portrait painted by David Rent Etter between 1829 and 1837.

Militia. So did his older brother Rezin. They served in the Second Division, a consolidation of the Seventeenth through the Nineteenth Regiments, encompassing volunteer companies from the parishes of Avoyelles, Catahoula, Natchitoches, and Rapides. Most of the Tejanos who had fled Arredondo's wrath had taken refuge in Natchitoches. Many of them also enlisted in the militia.

Everybody's timing was off, however. The War of 1812 officially ended with the signing of the Treaty of Ghent on December 24, 1814. Unfortunately, news of the treaty had not reached the United States of America by January 8, 1815. On this day, the British army attacked the defenses of New Orleans, Louisiana. The Bowies' Louisiana regiment did not arrive in time to help General Andrew Jackson repel the British force.

Even though he had not fought in the battle

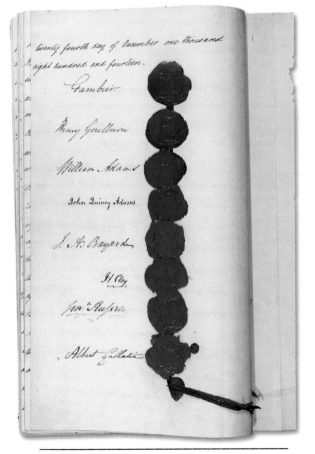

The Treaty of Ghent ended the War of 1812. American diplomats, including John Quincy Adams and Henry Clay, met British officials in the small town of Ghent, Belgium.

of New Orleans, Bowie's brief military career served as a rite of passage into manhood. After a brief visit with his parents back in Opelousas, James Bowie set out on his own. He acquired property some 25 miles (40.2 km) to the north along Bayou Bouef in southwestern Avoyelles Parish, Louisiana. There he engaged in a lumbering operation, clearing forests and selling the timber.

John remembered that James had grown into "a stout, rather raw-boned man, of six feet [1.8 m] height, [who] weighed 180 pounds [81.6 kg]." Since the average height of that era was about six inches (15.2 cm) less than it is now, Bowie towered over most other men. He was sometimes called Big Jim Bowie. His reddish brown hair formed a widow's peak on his high forehead. His piercing eyes gazed over a straight, almost pointed nose. In the style of the day, he wore long sideburns, which descended toward a cleft chin.

James Bowie was "about as well made as any man I ever saw," boasted his brother John. "Taken altogether he was a manly, fine-looking person, and by many of the fair ones he was called handsome."

Perhaps Big Jim Bowie, following the example of his brother, Rezin, enlisted in the next military expedition into Texas. In the spring of 1819, determined to liberate Texas from Spain, Dr. James Long raised a force of eighty men in Natchez, Mississippi. As he marched across Louisiana, his army swelled to three hundred men. Frontiersmen joined up. So did some of the Tejanos still

This portrait of Moses Austin is of disputed authenticity, but it is the only reputed likeness of Stephen F. Austin's father.

in exile. However, by that time many of the refugee Bexarenos had drifted home to San Antonio.

The rebel army easily captured Nacogdoches. On June 23, 1819, they again proclaimed Texas a republic, with Dr. Long as president. However, in October, five hundred Spanish troops arrived from Bexar and drove the rebels back into Louisiana. The new republic had been quickly crushed and its president exiled back to his native country.

If James Bowie had served in Dr. Long's army he, like Rezin, had missed the final defeat. Historical records placed him in Avoyelles Parish, Louisiana, in early October, about the time the Spanish soldados were marching against Long's rebels in Nacogdoches.

It would be left to the lead miner, Moses Austin, to open Texas through peaceful means, as he had done when he had gained entrance into Spanish Missouri. In December 1820, Austin journeyed to San Antonio de Bexar and received permission from the Spanish officials to bring American colonists into the sparsely populated province.

Moses Austin died shortly afterward. His son Stephen Fuller Austin, then twenty-seven years old, inherited his father's mission to colonize Texas.

# 3. Stupendous Schemes and Daring Enterprises

Whether or not James Bowie participated in Dr. Long's failed attempt to liberate Texas, Bowie had ventured into the Spanish province ahead of Moses Austin. Late in 1819, James and his brothers John and Rezin visited the pirate Jean Laffite at his new Galveston Island headquarters on the Texas coast. The Bowies were about to engage in the first of their notorious exploits. They would purchase slaves from Laffite to smuggle back into the United States to be sold at public auction.

Since its formation the United States had wrestled with the ethical question of the "peculiar institution," as slavery was called. For a long time, people had avoided thinking about the morality of it because it was so profitable to both the northern merchants, whose ships brought the enslaved Africans to the United States, and to the wealthy southern aristocrats who purchased the slaves to work on plantations. They also tried to justify slavery by saying that it had dated from prehistoric times. It was even mentioned in the Bible. Moreover, by 1800, slavery still existed in most of the world.

A newspaper advertisement believed to be from the 1780s announces the arrival of a cargo of slaves. About 250 slaves would be up for auction aboard the *Bance Island*, a boat docked in Charleston, South Carolina. In this ad, the slave traders claim that the slaves are healthy and are not infected with smallpox, a deadly disease.

In the late 1700s, a few Americans began to recognize the evils of slavery. Those who called for an end to slavery were called abolitionists.

In reality, the slave owners were almost as few in number as were the abolitionists. Most Americans had no need for slaves, and most could not afford slaves anyway. Sadly, most Americans at that time did not regard slavery as immoral.

In 1808, the government attempted a compromise to try to appease both the slave owners and the abolitionists. The compromise allowed slavery to remain legal, but the importation of new slaves into the country was outlawed.

However, the Louisiana Purchase five years earlier had created a tremendous demand for more slaves. They were needed to work the new sugar and cotton plantations that sprang up in the bayou lands of the new southwestern frontier. The critical shortage of slaves escalated their value. An average male slave began selling for more than one thousand dollars. That was enough money to generate a thriving black market for smugglers.

In 1820, the U.S. government classified the smuggling of slaves into the country as an act of piracy that carried the death penalty. The U.S. Navy patrolled the coastal waterways watching for ships carrying smuggled slaves. The law also offered a generous bounty on the smugglers. In Louisiana, if someone alerted the authorities to a smuggling operation, the slaves were confiscated, or taken, and were sold at public auction. Half of the sale price went to the parish and the other half went to the informer as a reward.

At Galveston, Laffite commanded his own fleet of pirate ships that preyed on vessels in the Gulf of Mexico and the Caribbean Sea. Along with the gold and silver they plundered, the pirates also captured shiploads of enslaved Africans bound for Brazil, Cuba, and the West Indies islands, where the importation of slaves was still legal. The pirates returned their booty, including the slaves, to Galveston Island in Spanish Texas, outside of U.S. jurisdiction.

Galveston Island probably did not have enough cells to imprison large numbers of captured slaves. Laffite eagerly offered to sell his contraband slaves at a fraction of their market value to smugglers who would take the risk of delivering the slaves to the United States.

John Bowie recalled the Bowie brothers' first venture to Galveston. They bought forty slaves from Laffite, "at a rate of one dollar per pound, or an average of $140 for each negro."

The Bowies were gambling their lives on a dangerous enterprise. The Texas coast was home to the hostile Karankawa Indians, a people well known for their cannibalistic rituals. Spanish soldados, on the alert since Dr. Long's failed expedition, patrolled the borderland. American troops were stationed across the boundary line. The Bowies had to sneak their forty slaves past the Karankawas and the soldiers and through the treacherous swamps that spanned the Texas-Louisiana border.

Despite its illegal nature, the Bowies' scheme also displayed their boldness and their cleverness. Back in Louisiana the brothers stashed the smuggled slaves and then immediately alerted the parish authorities to their location. The slaves were confiscated and sold at auction. The Bowie brothers could afford to outbid any other potential buyer, because they would regain half their cost as the reward for informing on the contraband slaves.

Then, with legal title, they could sell the slaves anywhere in the United States.

During 1820, the Bowies made several more slave-smuggling expeditions from Galveston Island to Louisiana. The local authorities must have realized the Bowie brothers' game. However, the authorities had no incentive to stop it since the parish also profited from the operation. The wealthiest and most prominent men in the region were grateful to acquire new slaves for their plantations. Though illegal, the operation did not seem immoral in an age that still tolerated the "peculiar institution." John Bowie wrote, "We continued to follow this business until we made $65,000, when we quit, and soon spent all our earnings."

William H. Sparks, a friend of the Bowie family, tried to explain the brothers' ambivalent sense of ethics:

> *They despised a petty thief, but admired Lafitte [sic] despised a man who would defraud a neighbor or deceive a friend, but would without hesitation co-operate with a man or party who or which aspired to any stupendous scheme or daring enterprise without inquiring as to its morality.*

In 1821, James's father, Reason Bowie, passed away on his land near Opelousas. That same year, Stephen F. Austin set out to fulfill his own late father's dream of colonizing Texas. Two prominent Bexarenos, Don Juan José

Erasmo Seguín and Juan Martín de Veramendi, met Austin at the border. Veramendi had been one of the refugees who had fled with his family to Louisiana. Seguín stubbornly had remained in Bexar during the dark days that followed the battle of the Medina. The Spanish general Arredondo had suspected that Seguín was loyal to the revolution and had confiscated his property, but Seguín had been spared the firing squad. Eventually Seguín won back his property in the courts, but he hated the Spaniards as much as did Veramendi.

The Bexarenos guided Austin toward San Antonio de Bexar. Even before the party reached Bexar they encountered some vaqueros, Mexican cowboys, who related that Mexico finally had won its revolution and had achieved independence from Spain.

The news excited Seguín and Veramendi. However, it required Austin to travel all the way to Mexico City, some 1,200 miles (1,931.2 km) overland. Spain, not Mexico, had given his father permission to colonize. After many months, Austin persuaded the new Mexican government to grant him permission to bring colonists into Texas.

In 1824, Mexico adopted a democratic constitution, patterned very closely after the U.S. Constitution. Along with the cheap lands available in Texas, this new democracy further encouraged U.S. citizens, already accustomed to self-government, to migrate into the province. "G. T. T." was carved onto the doors of abandoned cabins around the United States, alerting neighbors that the

residents had "Gone to Texas." Bankers inscribed those same three letters into their ledger books to explain debts that probably never would be repaid.

Texas was called the Land of Milk and Honey. It was the new frontier, the greener pasture that promised a new life or a new beginning. By 1830, some twenty thousand colonists flooded into the Mexican province, easily outnumbering the three thousand Tejanos who resided there. Anglo-American settlements sprang up along the Texas coastal plain, from Nacogdoches to the Colorado River.

Stephen F. Austin established the town of San Felipe de Austin on the Brazos River to serve as his headquarters. It became the unofficial Anglo capital of Texas. However, San Antonio de Bexar, on the western frontier, remained the seat of government. The westernmost of the new Anglo settlements, Gonzales, lay 80 miles (128.7 km) east of San Antonio.

James Bowie and his brothers did not immediately take advantage of the opportunities Texas offered. The Bowie brothers already were engaged in another lucrative, or moneymaking, enterprise. They had become land speculators, buying and selling vast acres (ha) of land across Louisiana and Arkansas. Unfortunately,

---

*Opposite*: Stephen F. Austin traveled to Mexico City, the seat of the Mexican government, to claim the right of Americans to settle in Texas. On this detail of an 1820s map made by David H. Burr for the U.S. House of Representatives, Mexico City is marked by a red rectangle.

James Bowie was known for his many forged claims. However, the document above is James Bowie's legitimate petition for land east of the Navidad River in present-day Colorado County, Texas, from Stephen F. Austin in 1831. Here he has signed his own name (see detail). In his forgeries, Bowie used many different names but officials became suspicious because he never tried to conceal his handwriting.

Historian William C. Davis suggested that James Bowie practiced land fraud on a grander scale than did anyone else, brazenly submitting false claims for title to approximately 65,000 Louisiana acres (26,304.6 ha) and another 60,000 acres (24,281 ha) in the Arkansas Territory. Davis based his estimates on speculation. He admitted that critical documents had been lost, and he also credited James Bowie with masterminding transactions in which Bowie's name never appeared.

However, at least one nineteenth-century U.S. land official believed that James Bowie did indeed conceal at least part of his land-fraud enterprise behind hired front men. The official identified Martin Despallier as one of the men who "made the claims known in our state as the Bowie claims." The true extent of James Bowie's land-fraud operation remains yet another Bowie mystery.

the historical evidence suggests that they sold a lot more land than they actually bought or owned.

The Louisiana Territory, which had been shuffled from Spain back to France and then to the United States, lent itself to land fraud.

The Bowies forged Spanish land grants for uncontested land in the public domain. Then they submitted the fake claim to the U.S. land office for approval. As with the slave operation, when legitimate title had been established, the brothers could sell the land for pure profit.

It was almost a victimless crime. No one was hurt except the U.S. government, which lost some tiny parcel of public land in the process.

Moreover, it was not technically a crime. Land fraud schemes were so new, the U.S. government had not yet enacted any laws or penalties against them. The only risk was that the land office might discover the forgeries and deny the claims.

In fact the land office did discover a large volume of forged land titles. They became lumped together as the "Bowie claims," and they kept land courts busy for many years.

# 4. Mr. Bowie with a Large Knife

Around 1824, James Bowie moved from Avoyelles Parish to neighboring Rapides Parish, near the town of Alexandria on the Red River. There Bowie renewed his friendship with Samuel Levi Wells III, who had served as a sergeant in the Louisiana Militia during the New Orleans campaign.

Wells belonged to a large, prominent family. His pioneer father, Samuel L. Wells II, had become the largest landowner in central Louisiana, and he had served in the state legislature. Dr. Richard Cuny and his brother, Samuel, first cousins of the Wells family, also owned large plantation estates in Rapides.

Samuel had another cousin, an orphan, named Cecelia Wells. Apparently she attracted the attention of James Bowie. He was then in his late twenties. All of his brothers were married. Many years later, Mrs. Elve Soniat du Fosset, granddaughter of Rezin P. Bowie, would claim that James and Cecelia were once engaged to be wed.

The Wells and Cuny families were in the middle of a hostile personal and political feud with some relative

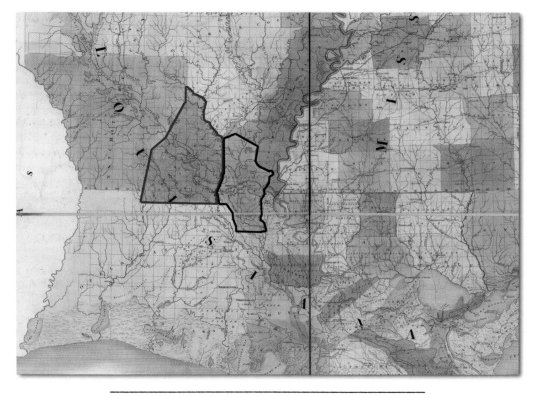

In 1824, Avoyelles Parish, outlined in blue on this 1839 map by David H. Burr, was a lush region of wandering bayous, cotton plantations, and sugarcane farms. Rapides Parish, outlined in red, lay to the northwest. In the north, rolling hills were covered with pine trees. In the south, low-laying swamps drained into the Red River.

newcomers to Louisiana. Colonel Robert Alexander Crain and the Blanchard brothers, Alfred and Carey, had arrived from Virginia. Major Norris Wright and Dr. Thomas Maddox were from Maryland.

The friends of Colonel Robert Crain described him as "the personification of chivalry." However, Crain was known to pay off his debts with a lead ball from a dueling pistol. As did Crain, Major Norris Wright enjoyed a reputation as a duelist. He was described as the best shot in the parish.

As a loyal friend of the Wells and Cuny families, James Bowie was drawn into the feud. On one occasion when Bowie requested a bank loan, Major Wright used his political influence to prevent it. Then, in 1826, James Bowie learned that Major Wright had been slandering Bowie's reputation. Enraged, Bowie stormed into Alexandria. He found Wright in the salon of Bailey's Hotel, playing cards with some friends. When Bowie confronted Wright, the local sheriff drew a pistol from under his coat and fired at Bowie. The pistol ball only grazed Bowie's ribs. Bowie had no weapon, but he threw himself upon Wright. As John Bowie later recalled, "Had Wright not been rescued by his friends James would have killed him with his fists."

The two men were separated, but they knew they would meet again. After that, James Bowie always carried a weapon. The single-shot pistols of that day were unreliable and often misfired. Although Bowie would carry one, his brother John wrote that James also "had a neat leather scabbard made for his hunting knife, and affirmed that he would wear it as long as he lived, which he did."

By all accounts it was an ordinary knife. The blade, forged from an old file, measured about 8 or 9 inches (20 or 23 cm) in length. The handle was made of wood scales. It looked like a butcher knife.

The political feud continued. In the local elections of January 1827, Samuel Wells III defeated Norris Wright

The origin of the first Bowie knife is yet another Bowie controversy. "The first Bowie-Knife was made by myself in the parish of Avoyelles," claimed Rezin P. Bowie. "The length of the knife was nine and one-quarter inches, its width one and a half inches, single edge, and blade not curved. . . ." Rezin continued:

Colonel James Bowie had been shot by an individual with whom he was at variance; and as I presumed that a second attempt would be made by the same person to take his life, I gave him the knife to be used as occasion might require, as a defensive weapon. Some times afterwards . . . it was resorted to by Colonel James Bowie in a chance medley, or rough fight, between himself and certain other individuals with whom he was then inimical, and the knife was then used only as a

*defensive weapon—and not until he had been shot
down; it was then the means of saving his life.*

Two of Rezin's grandchildren credited the actual making of the
knife to Jesse Clifft, who forged the knife under Rezin's supervision.
Both John J. Bowie and family friend Caiaphas Ham attributed the
manufacture of the knife to a Kentucky blacksmith named Lovel H.
Snowden. "[James] whittled a piece of wood into a model,"
wrote Ham. "A flat file was used in the making. When finished
it was not more than twelve inches long, handle and all."

The historical record reveals that Jesse Clifft went to Texas
around 1830. After his departure, Clifft's Louisiana property was
sold at public auction. The blacksmith from Kentucky, Lovel H.
Snowden, purchased the land, including Clifft's forge. Whether
Clifft or Snowden or Rezin Bowie himself made the first
Bowie knife remains yet another Bowie mystery.

for parish sheriff, and Sam Cuny gleefully triumphed over Colonel Robert Crain's bid for brigadier general of the militia. Later that year, Cuny and Crain exchanged shots at each other. Crain was wounded in the left arm. He recovered, vowing to shoot Cuny on sight.

The climax to all the animosity came on September 19, 1827. Dr. Thomas Maddox had related some insulting remarks about the character of Samuel Wells's sister, Mary Sibley. Such a breach of chivalry, or gentlemanly behavior, could only result in a duel between Wells and Maddox. They selected the first sandbar above Natchez, Mississippi, as their field of honor.

Five men, including James Bowie and Sam Cuny, accompanied Samuel Wells to the sandbar on that warm September day. Major George C. McWhorter served as Wells's second. By prior arrangement, only the duelists, their seconds, and their physicians would appear on the beach. As witnesses, Bowie and Cuny watched from a willow grove at the northwest end of the sandbar.

The Maddox party consisted of eleven men. Colonel Crain acted as Maddox's second. Major Norris Wright and the Blanchard brothers witnessed the affair from the trees at the southeast end of the beach.

At the appointed hour of noon, someone gave the signal to fire. Wells and Maddox raised their pistols and

---

*Previous spread:* The knife in this photo is believed to have been made by James Black of Washington, Arkansas. It is generally believed that Black made a knife for Bowie, though not necessarily his first knife.

exchanged shots. However, neither man was an experienced duelist. They both missed.

They instructed their seconds to reload their pistols so that, one more time, they might try to kill each other like gentlemen. Again, on the signal, they fired. Again they both missed.

At that point, Wells and Maddox determined that their honor had been satisfied. They shook hands. However, this peaceful resolution did not satisfy the mutual hatred of some of the witnesses.

With Bowie right behind him, Sam Cuny charged from the trees and confronted Crain, demanding that they settle their differences then and there. At that moment Crain held two loaded pistols, in case Wells and Maddox had desired a third exchange of fire.

Crain pointed a pistol at Cuny. Drawing his own pistol, Bowie stepped in front of Cuny as Crain pulled the trigger. The force of the pistol ball spun Bowie around. Bowie's shot went wild. As Cuny pulled his own pistol, Crain fired his second gun. Cuny fell to the sand, mortally wounded. He would bleed to death in a few minutes.

Somehow Bowie remained on his feet. He staggered toward Crain, who held two empty pistols. Crain threw one of them. It struck Bowie in the forehead, inflicting a bloody gash. Bowie dropped to his knees as Crain fled to the woods.

Suddenly it seemed that everyone was firing pistols. The affair of honor had turned into a desperate battle.

Through the blood that drained into his eyes, Bowie spotted Major Norris Wright and the Blanchard brothers racing toward him. Wright stopped and drew a pistol. At that moment someone placed a loaded pistol into Bowie's hand. Bowie and Wright exchanged shots. Bowie's pistol ball struck Wright in the left side. Bowie was hit in the left breast. Although both men were wounded, Bowie several times, their adrenaline and mutual animosity kept them fighting.

Wright discarded his empty pistol and pulled a lethal sword blade from his cane. Struggling to his feet, Bowie drew his knife from its scabbard. An eyewitness remembered that they "advanced on each other, Mr. Bowie with a large knife, and Major Wright with a sword cane. . . ."

Wright thrust his sword blade toward Bowie's chest. Bowie deflected the sword point into his arm and plunged his own blade into Wright's shoulder. Wright staggered back. Then Carey Blanchard fired at Bowie. Hit yet again, this time in the thigh, Bowie fell back to the sand. Samuel Wells reported what happened next:

> (Wright) and Alfred Blanchard drew their sword canes and commenced stabbing (Bowie); they had stabbed him several times before he could, after wonderful exertion, recover to his seat, but as soon as he attained that position, he made a grab at Wright who was still stabbing and caught him by the collar of his coat, drew him down, and at one desperate lunge plunged

*his butcher knife up to the handle in his breast, (Wright) died instantly without a groan or struggle—*

Then Bowie slashed his knife in a great arc. Alfred Blanchard staggered back, his side ripped open.

Neither Wells nor Maddox, the original duelists, had fired a shot in the melee. They had made their truce before the battle erupted. After most of the guns had been fired, they worked together to restore peace.

Incredibly only two men, Cuny and Wright, had been killed. Others were wounded, Bowie the most seriously.

In a letter written the day after the fight, Samuel Wells reported, "Bowie is shot through the lungs and thigh, and stabbed in seven places, the faculty [doctors] generally are of the opinion that he will not recover."

Somehow, James Bowie did recover. As newspapers circulated the story of the Sandbar Fight around the country, Bowie achieved an almost legendary status. His knife, which had been baptized in blood, was christened with its master's name. It became the first Bowie knife.

In 1828, Bowie made an exploratory trip into Texas, going at least as far as San Felipe. There he visited the blacksmith shop of Noah Smithwick. Smithwick recalled seeing the knife that Bowie had wielded on the sandbar:

*The blood christened weapon . . . was an ordinary affair with a plain wooden handle, but when Bowie recovered from his wound he had the*

The Sandbar Fight made Jim Bowie's knife at least as popular as its master. In June 1836, the Red River Herald of Natchitoches, Louisiana, reported that after the "dreadful conflict" that took place in Mississippi, "All the steel in the country was immediately converted into Bowie Knives." Certainly by the 1830s the Bowie knife had become standard equipment for anyone venturing into the wilderness. "The Bowie knife is the weapon most in vogue," observed Francis C. Sheridan, an English visitor to Texas in 1840. Sheridan further noted that many of the Bowie knives had been manufactured in Great Britain. In those early days any large knife, regardless of blade design, could be called a Bowie. Later the term became more specifically applied to single-edged knives possessing a cross-guard and a "clipped" point (in which a false edge angles down from the back of the blade to the point). Whether James Bowie himself popularized that design, or ever carried such a knife, is another unresolved mystery. Although many knives have surfaced accompanied by claims that they belonged to Big Jim Bowie, there is no absolute evidence to support them. However, his brother Rezin capitalized on the fame of the knife by presenting Bowie knives to his friends. Several of these knives still exist. One is on permanent display at the Alamo.

*precious blade polished and set into an ivory handle; the scabbard also being silver mounted. Not wishing to degrade it by ordinary use, he brought the knife to me in San Felipe to have a duplicate made. The blade was about ten inches long and two broad at the widest part.*

Returning to Louisiana, Bowie moved down to join brothers Rezin and Stephen and their mother, Elve, at their new Acadia plantation. It encompassed some 2,100 acres (849.8 ha) on Bayou La Fourche near Thibodaux. There they grew sugarcane and established one of the first steam-powered mills in Louisiana. If the story is true about James's engagement to Cecelia Wells, he probably planned to move Cecelia to Acadia after their wedding.

Tragically Cecelia succumbed to a fever in Alexandria on September 7, 1829. Rezin Bowie's granddaughter, Mrs. Elve Soniat du Fosset, wrote that Cecelia died "just two weeks previous to the day set for the wedding."

Perhaps her death was the reason Bowie left Acadia. Perhaps he was trying to get away from creditors who were trying to collect on his debts. Maybe, with the approaching new year, he needed a new beginning in a new place. Whatever the reason, in early 1830, James Bowie rode away with his friend Caiaphas Ham. They were "Gone to Texas."

They stopped briefly at San Felipe and probably presented letters of introduction to Stephen F. Austin, as this was the custom of the time. Austin was an honorable

man, determined to follow the laws of the Mexican government that had granted him permission to settle in
Texas. As the unofficial Anglo leader in Texas, and as a
close friend of the authorities in San Antonio de Bexar,
Austin was able to keep out anyone he considered
undesirable.

Certainly Austin had heard about James Bowie and
the vicious Sandbar Fight. Austin also probably had
heard of Bowie's dubious land transactions. Opposed to
both violence and land speculation, Austin should not
have liked Bowie. However, there was something about

Opened by the Spanish army in the 1680s, the Camino Real
later brought a flood of Anglo immigrants to Texas and Mexico.
This historic rancho, the Rancho de las Golondrinas, was an
important stopping point along this famous road.

the tall man with the big knife, the *cuchillo grande*, that appealed to Austin. Indeed, within a few years, Austin would find Bowie very useful.

After greeting Austin, Bowie and Ham continued west along the Camino Real, the old Spanish Royal Highway. They passed through Gonzales, the westernmost Anglo town, situated on the sleepy Guadalupe River. Eighty miles (129 km) farther west, they would find San Antonio de Bexar.

As they approached the town, they passed to the south of mission San Antonio de Valero, the old Spanish ruin that had been transformed into a makeshift fortress called the Alamo.

# 5. San Saba Silver

On reaching San Antonio, Ham remembered, he and Bowie "were treated with great consideration, courtesy, and hospitality" by Juan Martín de Veramendi and Don Erasmo Seguín. "Our sojourn in the 'war-worn city' was very pleasant," Ham continued. It must have been especially pleasant for James Bowie, because as Ham put it, "Bowie fell in love."

The object of Bowie's affection was Veramendi's daughter, Maria Ursula. At the age of two she had survived the frantic flight to Louisiana to escape Arredondo. Now eighteen years old, Ursula, as she was called, had grown into a refined Latin beauty. It also helped that she came from one of the wealthiest and most prominent families in Texas.

After an appropriate period of courtship, on April 25, 1831, James Bowie married Ursula in the San Fernando Church in San Antonio. Although it may have been a marriage of convenience, providing Bowie with money and prestige, all accounts report that Bowie and Ursula loved each other very much. One Texan, Captain William

According to their marriage certificate, James Bowie married Ursula de Veramendi at the San Fernando Church in San Antonio de Bexar on April 25, 1831.

G. Hunt, recalled:

*I first met Colonel Bowie and his wife at a party given them on the* Colorado *on Christmas Day, 1831. Mrs. Bowie was a beautiful Castilian lady, and won all hearts by her sweet manners. Bowie was supremely happy with her, very devoted and more like a kind and tender lover than the terrible duelist he has since been represented to be.*

Ursula's cousin, Juana Alsbury, described Bowie as
"a tall, well-made gentleman, of a very serious counte-
nance, of few words, always to the point, and a warm
friend." She added, "In his family he was affectionate,
kind, and so acted as to secure the love and confidence
of all." Other Bexarenos warmly embraced the large
American with the cuchillo grande, or big knife. Juan
Martín de Veramendi, who had been appointed vice
governor of the combined provinces of Texas and
Coahuila, treated Bowie more as a son than a son-in-
law. Together they built a cotton mill near Mission San
Jose. Bowie and Ursula moved into a house near the

After the invention of the cotton gin in 1793, cotton became
the foundation of America's economy. Cotton mills, like this one, were
used to manufacture cotton fibers.

mission. Bowie also entered into some land speculation around Monclova, Mexico.

Then James Bowie became captivated by another project, a daring enterprise that might make him more money than all of his other ventures combined. He would attempt to find the lost silver mines of the San Saba River.

Perhaps his Bexareno friends had related the history, and the legends, about the San Saba mines. In April 1757, the Spaniards had ventured 150 miles (241 km) northwest of San Antonio into hostile Indian territory to establish a mission and presidio along the San Saba River. On March 16, 1758, more than one thousand Comanche stormed the wooden stockade that enclosed the mission. The Comanche massacred most of the inhabitants and burned the mission structures to the ground. The presidio, built of limestone, endured another decade under a constant state of siege by the Indians. Then the hungry and exhausted soldados who had survived finally withdrew back to Bexar. That much was historical record.

However, there were tantalizing legends that during their brief stay on the San Saba, the Spaniards had discovered rich veins of silver ore in caverns along the river. The soldados had mined the silver and had concealed stacks of minted bars in underground chambers. Eighty years later, that fortune in silver still remained in the caves near the ruins of the old presidio, or so the legends claimed. Unfortunately, hostile Indians also remained along the San Saba River.

Undaunted, James Bowie mounted an expedition. His brother Rezin arrived from Louisiana to join him. They recruited their old friend, Caiaphas Ham. He would be especially valuable. During the previous few months Ham had been living and trading with a band of friendly Comanche. In fact Ham thought he might already have come close to discovering the lost mines. He reported:

> *One fat warrior was frequently my hunting companion. He pointed to a hill, and said—There is plenty of silver on the other side—We will go out by ourselves, and I will show it to you. If the other Indians find out I have done so they will kill both of us.*

However, the Comanche broke camp the next day and drifted on. Ham never saw the other side of the hill.

Six other men and two servant boys completed the expedition. They rode out of San Antonio on November 2, 1831, heading northwest toward the distant San Saba hills. Two weeks later they were nearing their destination when they encountered a small band of friendly Comanche en route to San Antonio.

From the Comanche, Bowie learned that a large war party of 124 Tawakonis, Waco, and Caddo were stalking his expedition, intent on taking the white men's horses, weapons, and scalps.

The Waco were sometimes hostile to groups of frontiersmen on
their lands. This 1834 portrait by George Catlin shows He Who
Fights with a Feather, chief of the Waco. Catlin said of his subject,
"I made a portrait of Ush-ee-kitz (He Who Fights With A Feather) . . .
a very polite and polished Indian, in his manners, and remarkable
for his mode of embracing the officers and others in council."

Bowie decided to try to reach the ruins of the old San Saba presidio, where the ancient stone walls would provide some cover. However, darkness closed in on them before they found the old Spanish fort. They had not seen any sign of hostile Indians. They made camp for the night in a grove of some thirty or forty live oak trees backed up against a creek to the west. A hill rose above the broken prairie to the northeast.

James Bowie reported that their campsite was 3 miles (4.8 km) north of the river. Rezin claimed they were 6 miles (9.6 km) from the presidio. Ham thought the presidio was 12 miles (19.3 km) away.

The next morning, November 21, as the expedition was breaking camp, the large war party appeared. Rezin and a man named David Buchanon walked out to try to treat, or negotiate, with the Indians. They were greeted by a hail of gunfire. Buchanon fell, wounded. Rezin carried him back to the trees.

The Indians circled behind the hill to the northeast and charged over its crest. The Texans were experienced frontiersmen who did not panic in the face of overwhelming odds. They aimed carefully, fired, and then shifted to another position. The charging Indians fired at the puffs of smoke emerging from the trees, but by that time the Texans had moved. Nonetheless, precious seconds were lost while they reloaded their single-shot flintlock rifles.

A mounted chief appeared at the top of the hill, urging

his warriors forward. Bowie called out to find out who was holding a loaded gun. Ham was.

Ham fired. The rifle ball ripped through one of the chief's lower legs and killed his horse. The chief extricated himself and hopped around on his one good leg, trying to protect himself behind a rawhide shield.

By then Bowie and others had reloaded. Their rifle balls tore through the painted symbols on the chief's shield and into the chief's body.

Indians closed around the fallen chief's body and carried it behind the hill. The rest of the warriors broke off their attack and retreated.

Within moments they were charging again. Again a chief appeared on the crest of the hill. Again Bowie asked who was loaded. Nobody was. A servant boy rushed up to Bowie with Buchanon's unfired rifle. Bowie aimed, fired, and the chief toppled from his horse. Again the Indians raced to their fallen chief and carried him back behind the hill.

Meanwhile some Caddo had crept into the creek behind the grove. They fired into the trees. The volley wounded a Texan named Matthew Doyle. Another Texan, Thomas McCaslin, fell dead. The surviving Texans shifted to the creek bank and shot down most of the Caddo. Soon the Indians tried a different tactic. They lit a fire, hoping either to force the Texans to retreat or to burn them out. Luckily the fire went out before it reached the creek.

A lull followed, during which the Texans erected a barricade of stone and timber. Then the Indians set fire to the prairie again. This time it worked. Raging flames swept directly toward the Texans. Bowie's men held their fire. The shower of sparks flying ahead of the blaze transformed every man's powder horn into a potential bomb. Uncapping their horns to charge their rifles was a risk that could cause a deadly explosion if a spark ignited the gunpowder. Worse, the Texans anticipated an attack under cover of the smoke. Rezin remembered that they determined to "place our backs together, draw our knives and fight them as long as any one of us was left alive."

However, the warriors did not charge. Instead they utilized the barrier of fire to drag their dead and wounded from the field.

As the blaze approached, the Texans grabbed their blankets and attacked the inferno, beating down the flames. The diminished fire swept through the grove. The Texans remained standing, their clothes charred, but still ready for a fight.

The warriors had had enough. With daylight waning they retreated behind the hill. All night long the Texans heard the Indians wailing over their dead. The next morning the Indians withdrew.

Bowie had lost one man, and three had been wounded. The Indians had suffered around fifty casualties. Bowie had also lost some horses and mules. Somehow he had to get his wounded back through hostile territory to San Antonio de Bexar.

The small band of friendly Comanche that had warned Bowie of the war party had arrived in San Antonio. They reported that Bowie's small expedition was about to be attacked by 124 Indians. It seemed impossible for nine men to hold off so many warriors. Everyone in the town concluded that Bowie and his men would be slain. The news devastated Ursula, and the Bexarenos mourned with her.

On the night of December 6, 1831, James Bowie and his men stumbled back into San Antonio. "There was not one of the party but had his skin cut in several places, and numerous shot-holes through his clothes," noted Rezin. Their return triggered a boisterous celebration in the town and a warm reunion between Bowie and Ursula.

James Bowie may not have found the lost silver mines, but the San Saba Indian battle further enhanced his reputation as a fighter and a leader of men.

# 6. On to Bexar!

Jim Bowie's San Saba fight was not the only battle between the Texans and the Native Americans. Amerind tribes often raided the colonial and Tejano settlements, usually to steal horses. Once a large Comanche war party burned down Gonzales. After the town was rebuilt, the Mexican authorities at San Antonio de Bexar provided the citizens of Gonzales with a small cannon for defense against the Indians.

However, a greater conflict loomed below the border. Revolution plagued the new republic of Mexico. The ensuing conflict existed between the federalists, who supported the Constitution of 1824, and the centralists, who advocated virtually dictatorial powers for their leader. Although the fighting was taking place in the area south of Texas, most Texans and Tejanos openly sympathized with the federalists and their leader, General Antonio López de Santa Anna.

The young lieutenant from Arredondo's army had displayed his courage at the battle of the Medina, and later he had risen to the rank of captain. As the Mexican

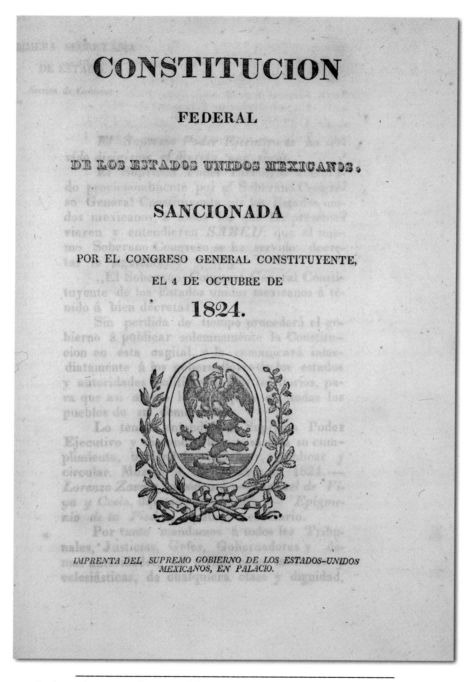

**CONSTITUCION**

FEDERAL

DE LOS ESTADOS UNIDOS MEXICANOS,

SANCIONADA

POR EL CONGRESO GENERAL CONSTITUYENTE,

EL 4 DE OCTUBRE DE

**1824.**

*IMPRENTA DEL SUPREMO GOBIERNO DE LOS ESTADOS—UNIDOS MEXICANOS, EN PALACIO.*

With the adoption of a Republican constitution in 1824, Mexico realized its dream of self-government. The constitution abolished slavery and gave all men the right to vote. However, the new government faced difficulties as rival political groups clashed and the economy suffered.

rebellion from Spain continued, Santa Anna displayed his political shrewdness. One day he defeated several thousand Mexican rebels and received a battlefield promotion to lieutenant colonel. However, shortly afterward he defected to the Mexican army, which had offered to make him a full colonel. Then, in the political revolts that had followed the establishment of the Mexican republic, Santa Anna had shifted from centralist to federalist and had achieved the rank of general. His changing political allegiances suggested one of two things. Either Santa Anna had been drifting toward a more democratic philosophy, or else he had no loyalty to any cause other than Santa Anna's.

This portrait of Stephen F. Austin was painted by an unknown German artist in New Orleans in 1836 for Austin's sister, Mrs. Emily Perry.

By 1832, the political tensions had spread across the border into Texas. Colonel José de las Piedras, commandant of the Mexican garrison at Nacogdoches, was a centralist. When he saw Texan sentiment growing against him, he attempted to disarm the colonists there. The Texans hastily gathered a force together.

Informed of the situation, Stephen F. Austin decided he wanted someone to take control at Nacogdoches and quickly resolve the conflict. He sent a rider to advise James Bowie that "his services were greatly needed."

On August 2, 1832, open conflict broke out at Nacogdoches between the Texan militia and the Mexican forces under Piedras. Both sides, numbering about three hundred men each, took cover in the buildings in the town. The battle continued into the evening, when Bowie arrived in town.

During the night Colonel Piedras withdrew his army into the dark woods and began retreating to the south. While other Texans debated a course of action, Bowie raised a force of twenty volunteers and galloped boldly in pursuit of the Mexicans.

Without being detected, Bowie circled around through the forest in front of Piedras's slower-moving army. When Piedras arrived at the Angelina River, his soldados were met by a volley of Texan rifle fire from the trees on the opposite bank. As brazen as ever, Bowie demanded that the Mexicans surrender. Piedras feared that the Texan militia from Nacogdoches was in close pursuit. Bowie gambled that Piedras did not know how few men blocked his retreat. The gamble worked. Nearly three hundred soldados surrendered to Bowie's twenty Texans.

James Bowie supplied the prisoners with food and provisions. They were marched to the border and then released. Stephen F. Austin was delighted that Bowie had resolved the conflict so efficiently and with minimal bloodshed.

Sam Houston, here in an 1840 portrait believed to be by George Catlin, would lead Texas in its fight for independence and would become the first president of the Republic of Texas in 1836.

That December, James Bowie passed through San Felipe. There Big Jim encountered one of the few men he ever had to look up to. Newly arrived in Texas, Sam Houston was a giant, bearlike man. A former governor of Tennessee, Houston also was a blood brother of the Cherokee, and he often seemed more comfortable among Native Americans than he did in the white man's society.

Big Jim Bowie guided Sam Houston to San Antonio de Bexar. The two men, both legends, became close friends along the way.

Back home in Bexar, Bowie hardly had time to visit with Ursula. Her father, now Governor Veramendi, needed Bowie's help in Saltillo, the capital of the combined provinces of Texas and Coahuila.

Santa Anna had triumphed in the revolution and

had won the popular election to become president of the republic of Mexico. However, political strife and violence continued in Saltillo, a centralist stronghold. Governor Veramendi was leading a movement to relocate the capital to Monclova, 100 miles (161) closer to the Texas border. In the meantime, in that dangerous environment, he needed the protection of James Bowie and his cuchillo grande.

Bowie reached Saltillo on February 7, 1833. With Bowie's assistance, Governor Veramendi persuaded the legislators to move the capital to Monclova.

Bowie returned to San Antonio. Again there was hardly time to unpack his saddlebags. A letter arrived from Louisiana. Rezin's eyesight was failing. Nearly blind, he needed his brother, James, to escort him to New York and Philadelphia to visit some eye specialists.

Of course Bowie would go. He always responded whenever anyone needed him. However, he had not always been there for the one person who needed him the most. Bowie loved Ursula more than anyone, but he had been away from her for almost half of the two years of their marriage.

At least this time Bowie was not charging off into some deadly battle against overwhelming odds. They should be able to spend time together when he returned. In the meantime she and her mother would join Governor Veramendi in Monclova.

Bowie drew up this contract to pay dowry to Ursula Veramendi on April 22, 1831 in Bexar. It would serve as a will if he died. He was 32. When he fell ill in Natchez in October 1833 he made revisions to his will in case he did not survive. Of course, he did not yet realize that his wife had died in a cholera epidemic in September.

The doctors in the northeast were able to restore only a small amount of Rezin's sight. The Bowie brothers returned to Louisiana in late September 1833. It was a dangerous time. A dreadful cholera epidemic was ravaging the lower Mississippi valley.

However it was malaria, not cholera, that struck Bowie. In Natchez, he fell so ill that he dictated his will on October 31. Bowie recovered, as he had done in Natchez six years earlier after the Sandbar Fight.

In the meantime the cholera epidemic swept through Texas and into Mexico. Thousands died. In Monclova alone, 571 people perished in the first half of September. Tragic news soon reached José Antonio Navarro in San Antonio. On September 26, Navarro sadly composed a letter to Samuel Williams, the government secretary in San Felipe. Navarro wrote:

> On my part, it has been a misfortune that my brother Veramendi; my sister, Josefa, his wife; and Ursulita Bowie have died in an awful way in Monclova.

> I have lost my special brother-in-law in Veramendi and Texas has lost a good son; a faithful and interested friend. . . .

> Bowie no longer has a wife and I hope some way he will be told of this news.

A letter bearing news of Ursula's death reached Bowie around mid-November. It nearly sent him into a relapse. Wearily he journeyed back to San Antonio. There, in the house that he and Ursula had shared, Bowie learned how deafening silence can be.

However, fate did not allow him much time to mourn. In Mexico City, President Santa Anna suddenly transformed from a federalist back to a centralist. He overthrew the Constitution of 1824 and proclaimed himself a dictator. He called himself the Napoléon of the West.

Again the federalists rose up in rebellion, and again

Above is an engraving showing the Inauguration ceremonies for Antonio López or Santa Anna.

civil war erupted in Mexico. Santa Anna launched his troops against the rebels, making a special example of the province of Zacatecas, which had the largest federalist force. After defeating the federalists and executing many of the rebels, Santa Anna allowed his troops to plunder the city of Zacatecas for two days. There were estimates that the province suffered as many as 2,500 casualties.

Stephen F. Austin, who had always opposed conflict between his colonists and the Mexican government, journeyed to Mexico City to meet with Santa Anna. Instead of securing peace, Austin was imprisoned in a Mexican dungeon for more than a year. Upon his return to Texas in September 1835, even Austin conceded, saying, "War is our only recourse."

However, Austin and his followers believed that the Texans should join with the Mexican revolutionaries, should overthrow Santa Anna, and should restore the Constitution of 1824.

Sam Houston, Henry Smith, and others, including James Bowie, argued that it was time for Texas to follow the example of the thirteen colonies and of Mexico itself. Texas should declare independence and become a republic.

Santa Anna recognized that Texas, with its large Anglo population, posed a serious threat. Most of the colonists were only one generation removed from the men who had fought and bled for liberty in the American Revolution. Worse, by 1835 there remained only two

Mexican garrisons in Texas, at San Antonio and at Goliad.

Santa Anna dispatched his brother-in-law, General Martín Perfecto de Cos, to lead five hundred troops into Texas. General Cos arrived by sea in mid-September 1835 and began marching toward San Antonio de Bexar.

In anticipation of the arrival of General Cos and his men, Colonel Domingo de Ugartechea, the Mexican commander at San

At Santa Anna's orders, General Martín Perfecto de Cos, here in an 1849 engraving by John Frost, led 300 men into Texas in September 1835. Cos dismissed the legislature of Coahuila and Texas, then in session in Monclova. He marched on to San Antonio, where he established his headquarters and prepared to do battle.

Antonio de Bexar, attempted to disarm the Texans. He sent a hundred soldados from the Alamo Company to confiscate, or seize, the small cannon at Gonzales, the nearest Texan settlement, 80 miles (128.7 km) to the east. However, the citizens of that town refused to surrender their cannon. Instead, 150 Texans attacked the soldados on October 2, 1835.

The tiny cannon boomed. One soldado died, and the others fled back to San Antonio. That tiny skirmish served as the "Lexington of Texas." It ignited the Texas Revolution.

One week later another force of Texans compelled the Mexican garrison at Goliad to surrender. That left only San Antonio de Bexar. Cos had just arrived there, increasing the number of soldados that defended the town to 650.

"On to Bexar!" became the battle cry of enthusiastic Texans drunk on both whiskey and victory. They elected Stephen F. Austin as their commander. On October 12, General Austin led his rowdy militia, three hundred strong, to the west. The Texan force arrived at Cibolo Creek,

*The small battle at Gonzales, which launched the Texas revolution, was called the Lexington of Texas. This was a reference to the battle that began the American Revolution. American colonies had protested various actions by British parliament. In response to some of these protests, the British sent troops to confiscate ammunition at Lexington and Concord. The colonists were warned by several express riders, including Paul Revere, and were able to send militia to defend the two towns. The first shot of the American Revolution was fired on April 19, 1775.*

only 20 miles (32.2 km) east of Bexar, on October 16. They camped there for several days.

On October 19, James Bowie rode into the Texan camp. He already held the rank of a militia colonel, which had been bestowed on him at Nacogdoches. Austin eagerly appointed Bowie as his aide de camp.

As the Texans continued their advance toward San Antonio, their numbers swelled to 450 volunteers. Austin placed Colonel Bowie in command of Captain James Walker Fannin's company of approximately fifty men. Austin instructed Bowie to scout ahead, to secure any provisions, and to determine the best approach to Bexar.

On October 24, Bowie's Texans defeated a small Mexican force near Mission Espada. The soldados retreated into Bexar. Austin arrived with the main body of his army on October 27 and camped at Espada. He added Captain Robert Coleman's company to Bowie's scouting party, giving Bowie about ninety men. Then Austin again sent Bowie ahead to "select the best and most secure position that can be had on the river, as near Bejar [Bexar] as practicable to encamp the army tonight. . . ."

Noah Smithwick, the San Felipe blacksmith, served under Bowie. Smithwick recalled:

> *We went on up, made our observations, and*
> *camped in a bend of the river on the east side,*
> *about a quarter of a mile above the old mission of*
> *Concepción and distant some two miles [3.2 km]*

*from San Antonio, expecting the main army to
follow right on, but for some reason Colonel
Austin did not do so.*

Night had fallen by the time Austin learned of Bowie's position. Austin did not want to risk moving his army in the darkness. Bowie was on his own at least until the next day.

Unfortunately, a spy had reported Bowie's presence to General Cos. Early the next morning, October 28, Cos dispatched Colonel Ugartechea with three hundred soldados and two artillery pieces to capture the advance force of Texans.

A thick fog masked the approach of the Mexican troops. However some Texas sentries heard the enemy advancing and raised a warning.

As the fog lifted, Colonel Ugartechea realized that Bowie had selected his campsite wisely. The Mexican infantry had to march across an open prairie into a withering crossfire of Texan rifles defending the horseshoe bend of the river.

A Texan named Creed Taylor recalled that "Bowie urged the boys to be cool and deliberate and to waste no powder and balls, but to shoot to hit."

Three times the Mexicans advanced. Three times the Texans drove them back. Creed Taylor remembered:

*When they were driven back the third and
last time, and while their officers were vainly*

*trying to rally them on their colors, which had been placed on the cannon, Jim Bowie shouted, "The cannon, boys! Come on and let's take the cannon." And with a wild cheer the men rushed forward, seized the color standard, wheeled the gun, which was loaded, and turned it on the enemy who fled in the direction of San Antonio. The fight was over.*

The Mexicans suffered about seventy casualties. One Texan had been killed and another wounded. Once again James Bowie had triumphed over superior odds.

General Cos would not again risk sending his troops outside the barricades that surrounded San Antonio. When Austin arrived with the main body of the army, the Texans settled in for a long siege.

On November 3 at San Felipe, political leaders from around Texas met at a convention that was called the Consultation. The men appointed Henry Smith as provisional, or temporary, governor of Texas and Sam Houston as commander in chief of the Texas army. Because the Texans besieging San Antonio were volunteers, who traditionally elected their own commander, Houston had no real authority over them. The Consultation instructed him to raise a regular army. The Consultation also appointed Stephen F. Austin, Texas's most able diplomat, as an ambassador to the United States with instructions to secure money and weapons for the revolution. The Consultation concluded with a call for another convention to meet March 1, 1836, at Washington-on-the-Brazos.

Upon Austin's departure for the United States, Edward Burleson assumed command of the Texan army at Bexar. On November 26, the legendary Texan scout Erastus "Deaf" Smith alerted Burleson that a Mexican pack train was approaching the town. The Texans suspected that the pack mules carried silver coins, payment for the besieged soldados at Bexar. Burleson dispatched Bowie with forty cavalrymen to intercept the pack train.

Bowie attacked and captured the pack train from its escort of one hundred Mexican dragoons. However, when Bowie's knife slashed into a pack, cut grass rather than silver coins tumbled onto the ground. Instead of silver for the soldados, the pack train was delivering fodder for the starving horses in the town.

Nonetheless, the Grass Fight, as it came to be known, energized the Texans. On December 5, 1835, they finally stormed San Antonio. The battle lasted for four days. By December 9, General Cos had withdrawn his forces from the city into the Alamo. On the next day he surrendered.

The Mexican prisoners were sent back into the interior of

Dragoons were mounted soldiers. They attacked on horseback and, when necessary, retreated on foot. This lithograph of a dragoon was done in 1828 by Claudio Linati.

Mexico under pledge that they would never again take up arms against the Constitution of 1824. With their departure there were no more santanistas, or followers of Santa Anna, in Texas. Naively, many of the Texan volunteers assumed the war was finished. They drifted home to their farms and families.

However, the war had barely begun. Already Santa Anna had assembled a massive army numbering some seven thousand men. Already he was preparing to march north, recapture Texas, and kill anyone, Texan or Tejano, who opposed him.

# 7. Remember the Alamo!

When General Sam Houston learned that Santa Anna was planning an invasion, Houston assumed that the Napoléon of the West would take the most direct overland route into the Texan colonies. That route led through Goliad, 90 miles (144.8 km) to the southeast of San Antonio de Bexar. Therefore Houston saw no strategic reason for trying to defend Bexar.

"I have ordered the fortifications in the town of Bexar to be demolished," Houston wrote Governor Henry Smith on January 17, 1836, "and if you think well of it, I will remove all the cannon and other munitions of war to Gonzales and Copano, blow up the Alamo, and abandon the place, as it will be impossible to keep up the Station with volunteers."

The man Houston had sent to San Antonio with those instructions was James Bowie. Houston advised Smith, ". . . there is no man on whose forecast, prudence, and valor I place a higher estimate than Colonel Bowie."

Riding at the head of thirty volunteers, Bowie arrived in San Antonio on January 18. Lieutenant Colonel James

Clinton Neill was now in command there, but his army had dwindled to less than one hundred men. Their only military advantage was the eighteen functional cannons they had captured from General Cos. It was the largest collection of artillery west of the Mississippi. The cannons could not be abandoned at Bexar to fall back into enemy hands. However, Bowie could not locate enough horses, mules, or oxen to move the artillery to the east.

Then Bowie received important intelligence. Santa Anna already had two thousand soldados on the Rio Grande and another five thousand troops marching to reinforce them.

". . . they intend to make a descent on this place in particular, and there is no doubt of it," Bowie wrote Governor Smith on February 2.

"The salvation of Texas depends in great measure in keeping Bejar out of the hands of the enemy," Bowie added. "Colonel Neill and myself have come to the solemn resolution that we will rather die in these ditches than give up this post to the enemy."

It was bold talk considering the overwhelming odds the Texans faced. Bowie added a postscript:

> *Our force is very small . . . only one hundred and twenty officers & men. It would be a waste of men to put our brave little band against thousands.*

Bowie already realized that the town could not be

defended with his small force. Only the previous month, the Texans had captured San Antonio from Cos, who commanded more than six hundred soldados. Bowie had a fraction of that number of men. The Texans would have to entrench themselves across the river in the Alamo.

The old mission compound had been built in the shape of an irregular rectangle. The main gate was located in the south wall, which was built of limestone. Flanking the entrance was a row of small rooms known as the low barracks.

General Cos's Mexican engineers had erected a lunette, a semicircular breastwork of timber, outside of the gate to fortify the entrance further. They also had closed a gap between the south wall and the church with a chest-high wooden palisade, or fence.

The old mission church, which jutted out to the south-

More than 100 years after Bowie's death, archaeologists began to study the Alamo. They found defensive trenches and temporary structures, scattered stones, bones, broken bottles, ceramic objects, and other artifacts. This rifle, held at the Alamo museum and library, belonged to David Crockett, a defender of the Alamo along with Bowie.

The former mission San Antonio de Valero is more commonly called the Alamo, named for Alamo de Parras, the company of Spanish mounted lancers who occupied San Antonio between 1803 and 1835. This is a view that was created by Edward Everett in 1847 of the Alamo church.

east, was the strongest building in the compound. It had stone walls 4 feet (1.2 m) thick. However, the church had never been completed. Although there were ceilings over the small rooms, a roof had never been constructed over the main portion of the church.

North of the church stood the two-story convent building, also built of stone. Priests had lived there when they were converting the Amerind tribes. The Texans called it the long barracks. Its upstairs rooms served as their hospital.

The rest of the walls enclosing the Alamo compound were made of adobe. Through long years of neglect the mud bricks had started to crumble. The north wall, especially, was in poor condition. What remained of it was leaning outward and was in danger of collapsing. Green B. Jameson, who served both as Bowie's aide and as the Alamo's chief engineer, braced the wall with vertical timbers and filled in the gaps with horizontal logs. In a letter to Houston, Jameson complained that "the Alamo was not built by a military people as a fortress . . . ."

However, the Alamo's greatest weakness was neither its design nor its state of disrepair. Those crumbling walls enclosed nearly 3 acres (1.2 ha) of land. Fitting an appropriate cannon crew to each piece of artillery required more than half of the Texan force. Only a handful of riflemen were left to defend a perimeter that extended more than ¼ of a mile (.4 km). The Texans would need at least five hundred men to garrison the Alamo adequately.

Already Governor Smith had authorized Lieutenant Colonel William Barret Travis, a twenty-six-year-old lawyer originally from South Carolina, to raise a force of one hundred men and to reinforce the Texans at Bexar. Travis recruited only thirty men. They arrived in San Antonio during the first week of February.

A few days later a force only half that size drifted into Bexar. They called themselves the Tennessee Mounted Volunteers in honor of a man who had joined their company in Nacogdoches. His name was David Crockett. The famed backwoods congressman, now 49 years old, had left Tennessee after a humiliating political defeat. He had told his constituents, the people in his congressional district, that they could go to heck, he was bound for Texas. At San Augustine, Texas, on January 9, Crockett dispatched a last letter back to his family:

> *I had rather be in my present situation than to be elected to a seat in Congress for life. I am in great hope of making a fortune for myself and my family, bad as my prospects has been.*

He closed the letter: "Do not be uneasy about me, I am among friends. . . . Your affectionate father. Farewell." Then he joined the small volunteer company and rode to the Alamo.

"We are now one hundred and fifty strong," Green B. Jameson wrote to Governor Henry Smith on February 11. "Col Crockett & Col Travis both here & Col Bowie in command of the volunteer forces."

Colonel Neill had left Bexar the day before to tend to ailing family members and to raise money for the Alamo garrison. His departure created a conflict of command. Both Neill and Travis were officers in the regular army, so Neill had relinquished his command to Travis. However, the vast majority of the garrison were volunteers who reserved the right to elect their own leader.

Crockett wisely sidestepped the dispute. His rank as colonel was only an honorary title anyway. "I have come to aid you all that I can in your noble cause," he told the Texans, "and all the honour that I desire is that of defending as a private . . . the liberties of our Common country. . . ."

Travis agreed to allow the men to select their new commander. The vote favored Big Jim Bowie. That night Bowie and the men celebrated in the streets of San Antonio.

The next day, after he had recov-  ered from the festivities, Bowie realized that this was no time for his and Travis's egos to inter- fere with their mutual cause. Bowie met with Travis and they agreed to share joint command.

Davy Crockett entertained the men with his humor. Sometimes he would pit his fid- dle in a noisy duel against the bagpipes of a Scottish defender named John McGregor. It all helped to raise the morale of the Alamo garrison.

William Barret Travis, an attorney from South Carolina, moved to Texas in 1831. He was only 26 years old when he arrived at the Alamo in February 1836. This 1835 drawing by Wiley Martin is the only known like- ness of Barret made from life.

By this time James Bowie's morale needed raising. Bowie had contracted a fever, an enemy that even his big knife could not intimidate. It was

Even before the Alamo, David Crockett, here in an 1831 watercolor by James H. Shegogue, was an American legend. Books, plays, and serial comics related his adventures.

lung related, possibly tuberculosis, pneumonia, typhoid, or some combination thereof. Dr. John Sutherland described James Bowie's disease as "being of a peculiar nature . . . not to be cured by an ordinary course of treatment." It hardly mattered. Virtually no medical supplies existed in Bexar. Moreover, Bowie could not afford to rest and recuperate. There was so much to be done.

Then, on February 23, the vanguard of Santa Anna's Army of Operations descended on Bexar. The Texans scrambled into the Alamo and watched over its western ramparts as approximately 1,500 soldados filed into the town across the river. Already the Texans were outnumbered ten to one, and the majority of the Mexican army had yet to arrive.

Santa Anna demanded that the Texans either surrender "or be put to the sword." Travis responded with a cannon shot. They would never surrender or retreat.

Infuriated, Santa Anna raised a blood-red banner

from the bell tower of the San Fernando church, the highest point in the town. The Texans knew the meaning of that red flag. Santa Anna would take no prisoners.

Then Santa Anna began positioning his artillery and began a cannonade that extended into the night. The next morning, Bowie finally collapsed from his illness. He turned over full command of the garrison to Travis. For the rest of the siege, he remained in his small, cell-like room in the low barracks near the gate. Lying in his cot, Bowie drifted in and out of a delirious fever.

The next day Travis wrote to Sam Houston, who, along with fifty-eight other delegates, soon would be assembling at the convention scheduled for March 1 at Washington-on-the-Brazos. The letter read, in part:

> *Our numbers are few and the enemy still continues to approximate his works to ours. I have every reason to apprehend an attack from his whole force very soon; but I shall hold out to the last extremity; hoping to secure reinforcements in a day or two. Do hasten on aid to me as rapidly as possible, as from the superior number of the enemy, it will be impossible for us to keep them out much longer. If they overpower us, we fall a sacrifice at the shrine of our country, and we hope posterity and our country will do our memory justice.*

Captain Juan Seguín, the son of Don Erasmo Seguín,

commanded a company of Tejanos who were defending the Alamo's walls. Travis selected Juan Seguín to carry the letter through the enemy lines. According to one story, Bowie insisted that Seguín take Bowie's horse, because it was the best mount in the Alamo.

As the siege progressed, Travis sent out other dramatic appeals for reinforcements. However, the only substantiated relief that the Alamo received was thirty-two men from the nearby town of Gonzales. They slipped past the Mexicans and into the Alamo shortly after midnight on March 1.

Two days later another thousand soldados marched into San Antonio to reinforce the Mexican army. Travis sensed that time was running out. That evening he wrote in a letter:

> . . . I feel confident that the determined valour and desperate courage, heretofore evinced by my men, will not fail them in the last struggle, and although they may be sacrificed to the vengeance of a Gothic enemy, the victory will cost the enemy so dear, that it will be worse for him than a defeat.

In the predawn hours of Sunday, March 6, the thirteenth day of the siege, Santa Anna launched his forces against the Alamo's walls. The Napoleon of the West concentrated more than one thousand soldados against the Alamo's crumbling north wall. Travis had placed

A popular legend relates that late in
the siege of the Alamo, Travis assembled
the men in the compound. He told them that
reinforcements would not reach the Alamo
in time, and he offered the volunteers the
chance to escape to safety. Drawing his
sword, Travis etched a line in the sand.
Then he asked that all who were willing to
stay and fight to the death cross over the line.

Every man stepped over the line except two.
James Bowie was too weak to rise
from his cot, but he asked if some of
the men would carry him across.

That left only a Frenchman, Louis Rose.
He was called Moses because, at 55,
he was one of the oldest men in the garrison.
Rose chose to leave. He scrambled over the
walls and disappeared into the night, surviving
to tell the legend of the Alamo's line in the sand.

himself at that post of honor. He died there, from a wound caused by a musket ball through his head. The Mexicans scrambling up the wall literally entered the Alamo over his dead body.

Once the walls were breached, most of the Texans retreated into the buildings. The soldados proceeded, room by room, through the Alamo compound. For the most part it was desperate, hand-to-hand combat in the terrible chaos of darkness and smoke.

When the Mexicans reached the south wall they burst into James Bowie's room. In a nearby room, eight-year-old Enrique Esparza huddled with his mother, his three brothers, and his sister. Enrique's father, Gregorio, manned a cannon defending the Alamo church. Enrique reported that Bowie:

> . . . *fired his weapons until his foes closed in on him. When they made their final rush upon him, he rose up in his bed and received them. He buried his sharp knife into the breast of one of them as another fired the shot that killed him.*

That is the popular image of Jim Bowie's death. In truth, Enrique Esparza probably did not actually see Bowie die. There are many other stories describing his death, but none of them come from reliable eyewitnesses. Perhaps Bowie was already dead before the Mexican bayonets and musket balls pierced his body. Perhaps he was

> *When news of the fall
> of the Alamo reached Louisiana,
> Bowie's elderly mother, Elve, allegedly
> remarked: "So Jim is dead. I'll wager they
> found no bullets in his back." She knew
> that her son would never be shot down
> while running from a fight.*

unconscious. However, if Big Jim Bowie were awake, and if he had had the strength to raise his arms, his fingers would have been wrapped around the butt of a pistol or the hilt of a knife.

Ultimately it hardly matters how Bowie and the other Texans died. They gave their lives for Texas, and Texas would remember them. "What not for country!"

By daybreak the terrible battle was finished. True to his word, Santa Anna had killed all of the Alamo garrison. He spared only about fifteen noncombatants. The Esparza family survived, as did the wives and children of some of the other Tejano and Texan defenders. So did

Travis's twenty-one-year-old slave, Joe.

Travis had kept his word as well. The Alamo had inflicted casualties on nearly a third of the Mexican assault force. A Mexican officer, Colonel Juan Almonte, remarked that "another such victory would ruin them."

One of the most common misconceptions about the Alamo is that the thirteen-day siege provided time for Houston to raise an army. In fact during most of the Alamo siege Houston was attending the convention at Washington-on-the-Brazos. However, the defenders of the Alamo did buy time for the convention to declare the independence of Texas on March 2. Francisco Ruiz and José Antonio Navarro were among the men at the convention who signed their names to the document.

The convention reaffirmed Houston as commander in chief of the Texan forces. Houston left Washington-on-the-Brazos on March 6, the same day that the Alamo fell. Five days later he arrived at Gonzales, where some five hundred Texans, aroused by the plight of the Alamo, had assembled. For the very first time, Houston was in command of a Texas army.

The Napoleon of the West met his Waterloo on the plain at San Jacinto. On the afternoon of April 21, only six

---

*Previous spread*: Attacking Texans crash the Mexican barricades in this detailed panorama of the battle of San Jacinto by H.A. McArdle. Sam Houston leads the charge, waving his hat as he leaps from his wounded horse (left of center), while Santa Anna, in a white sombrero (center, right), gallops past a tent in full flight.

weeks after the Alamo massacre, General Sam Houston led his ragtag army, now swollen to more than nine hundred men, across the great grassy prairie to attack Santa Anna's superior force. In only twenty minutes, the Mexicans were routed and Texas independence was won. More than six hundred soldados were killed. Most of the rest, including Santa Anna, were captured. Houston suffered only nine dead and twenty-five wounded. It was one of the most incredible victories in history. Significantly, the battle cry that had inspired those Texans as they charged across the prairie was "Remember the Alamo!"

James Bowie contributed to the triumph at San Jacinto in more ways than with his martyrdom. In his memoirs, Sam Houston wrote that after the Texans had fired their weapons, they did not take time to reload, instead ". . . drawing forth their bowie-knives [they] literally cut their way" through the enemy to victory.

James Bowie and the fateful massacre at the Alamo are the stuff of legends. Bowie made a contribution to history that goes beyond embellished stories. Through courage, determination, and the spirit of a true frontiersman, Bowie lives on in memory as one of Texas's and America's greatest heroes.

# Timeline

| | |
|---|---|
| **1718** | Mission San Antonio de Valero, later called the Alamo, is established. |
| **1758** | On March 16, Comanche attack the San Saba mission. |
| **1776** | On July 4, the American colonies declare their independence from Great Britain. |
| **1782** | On March 8, Reason Bowie marries Elve Ap-Catesby Jones in Georgia. |
| **1785** | John Jones Bowie is born. |
| **1793** | On September 8, Rezin Pleasant Bowie is born. |
| **1796** | James Bowie is born. |
| **1797(?)** | Stephen Bowie is born in Logan County, Kentucky. |
| **1800** | Reason Bowie settles his family in Missouri. |
| **1803** | Reason Bowie moves his family into present-day Louisiana. |
| **1810** | Father Miguel Hidalgo initiates the |

Mexican Revolution.

The Bowie family finally settles near Opelousas in St. Landry Parish, Louisiana.

**1813**    On April 1, the first Republic of Texas is established.

On August 18, General Joaquín de Arredondo defeats the Republican Army of the North.

**1815**    On January 8, the Battle of New Orleans occurs.

**1819**    On June 23, Dr. James Long's expedition captures Nacogdoches and declares a second Republic of Texas. It will be crushed by Spanish forces in October.

James Bowie and his brothers acquire slaves from the pirate Jean Laffite and smuggle them into the United States.

**1820**    In December Moses Austin secures permission to colonize Texas.

**1821**    Mexico declares independence from Spain.

Stephen F. Austin brings the first Anglo colonists into Texas.

**1824**    Mexico adopts a democratic constitution.

**1827**    On September 19, James Bowie kills Norris Wright in the Sandbar Fight.

**1830**    James Bowie leaves Louisiana and moves to Texas.

**1831**    On April 25, James Bowie marries Maria Ursula de Veramendi.

On November 21, James and Rezin Bowie, along with seven other men and two servant boys, repel 164 Native Americans near the San Saba River.

**1833**    Ursula Bowie dies of cholera.

Antonio López de Santa Anna overthrows the Constitution of 1824 and declares himself a dictator.

**1835**    On October 2, the Texans at Gonzales attack.

On October 24, James Bowie's men defeat a small Mexican force near Mission Espada, below San Antonio.

On October 28, James Bowie's men defeat three hundred soldados near Mission Concepción.

On November 26, the Grass Fight occurs.

On December 5, the battle of Bexar begins.

On December 10, General Cos surrenders the forces defending San Antonio de Bexar.

**1836**  On January 18, Bowie arrives in San Antonio with instructions from Sam Houston to destroy the fort there.

On February 2, Bowie explains the need to defend San Antonio.

On February 23, Santa Anna's army descends on San Antonio as the Texans take refuge in the Alamo.

On February 24, Colonel James Bowie collapses from illness.

On March 2, Texas declares itself an independent republic.

On March 6, Santa Anna's army storms the Alamo and massacres all the men.

On April 21, Texas gains independence.

# Glossary

**adrenaline** (uh-DREH-nuh-lin) A hormone secreted by the adrenal gland that stimulates the heart and increases muscular strength.

**ambivalent** (am-BIH-vuh-lint) Having simultaneous, conflicting emotions.

**Amerind** (A-muh-rind) Native American, literally a conjunction of American Indian.

**aristocrats** (uh-RIS-tuh-krats) Members of the wealthy upper class.

**Bexareno** (beks-uh-REE-no) A resident of San Antonio de Bexar. The population of San Antonio remained predominantly Hispanic until after the Texas revolution.

**brazen** (BRAY-zin) Audacious, or bold.

**breastwork** (BREST-werk) A hastily erected wall, usually only chest high, intended for defense.

**cannonade** (KA-nuh-nahd) A bombardment, a continuous firing of artillery.

**centralist** (SEN-truh-list) One who supports a strong, centralized government.

**chivalry** (SHIH-vul-ree) Noble qualities, such as courage, honor, and a readiness to help the weak.

**cholera** (KAH-luh-rah) A very contagious and often fatal intestinal disease.

**confiscate** (KON-fih-skayt) To legally take property away.

**contraband** (KON-truh-band) Illegal goods.

**dragoons** (druh-GOONZ) Heavily armed cavalry, sometimes described as mounted infantry.

**embellished** (em-BEH-lishd) Fictionalized a story so as to make it better.

**federalist** (FEH-duh-ruh-list) One who supports a union of states under a federal government.

**garrison** (GAR-uh-sun) A military post or the troops stationed there.

**knight errant** (NYT EHR-ant) A wandering knight seeking adventure.

**land grant** (LAND GRANT) Land given to an individual by a government.

**lucrative** (LOO-kruh-tiv) Producing wealth or profit.

**lunette** (loo-NET) A semicircular fortification that often protects the front or exterior of entranceways.

**malaria** (muh-LAR-ee-uh) A disease transmitted by a mosquito bite, which causes severe chills and fever.

**mission** (MIH-shun) A Spanish, fortlike compound where priests converted the Native American population to Catholicism.

**palisade** (pa-luh-SAYD) A fortification constructed from a row of pointed stakes set into the ground.

**phonetic** (fuh-NEH-tik) According to sound.

**presidio** (pruh-SEE-dee-oh) A Spanish fort, usually built to protect nearby missions.

**santanistas** (san-ta-NEE-stuhz) Followers of Santa Anna.

**Scottish dirk** (SKAH-tish DERK) A long, single-edged knife with a symmetrical blade tapering to a point. They were traditionally carried by ancient Scottish warriors.

**second** (SEH-kend) One that assists or supports another, especially in a duel.

**sojourn** (SOH-jern) A brief stay, a visit.

**soldado** (sohl-DAH-doh) The Spanish word for soldier.

**speculators** (SPEK-yoo-lay-terz) Those who engage in risky ventures for financial gain.

**Tejano** (tay-HA-no) A Hispanic resident of Texas.

**treat** (TREET) Negotiate, arrange a treaty.

**vaquero** (vuh-KEH-roh) A Mexican cowboy.

# Additional Resources

To learn more about James Bowie and the Alamo, check out these books and Web sites.

## Books

Flynn, Jean. *Jim Bowie: A Texas Legend*. Burnet, Texas: Eakin Publishers, 1980.

Gaines, Ann Graham. *Jim Bowie: Hero of the Alamo*. Berkeley Heights, New Jersey: Enslow Publishers, Inc., 2000.

## Web Sites

Due to the changing nature of Internet links, PowerPlus Books has developed an online list of Web sites related to the subject of this book. This site is updated regularly. Please use this link to access the list:
www.powerkidslinks.com/lalt/bowie/

# Bibliography

Batson, James L. *James Bowie and the Sandbar Fight*. Madison, WI: Batson Engineering and Metalworks, 1992.

Davis, William C. *Three Roads to the Alamo*. New York: HarperCollins Publishers, 1998.

Edmondson, J. R. *The Alamo Story—From Early History to Current Conflicts*. Plano, TX: Republic of Texas Press, 2000.

Hardin, Stephen L. *Texian Iliad*. Austin, TX: University of Texas Press, 1994.

Hopewell, Clifford. *James Bowie—Texas Fighting Man*.Austin, TX: Eakin Press, 1994.

Lord, Walter. *A Time to Stand*. New York: Harper & Brothers, 1961.

Smithwick, Noah. *The Evolution of a State or Recollections of Old Texas Days*. 1900. Reprint. Austin, TX: University of Texas Press, 1983.

Tinkle, Lon. *13 Days to Glory*. New York: McGraw-Hill Book Company, Inc., 1958.

# Index

# About the Author

A retired history teacher, J. R. Edmondson is the author of the book *The Alamo Story—From Early History to Current Conflicts*, and the booklet *Mr. Bowie With a Knife—A History of the Sandbar Fight*. His historical pageant, *Victory or Death*, was performed annually at the Alamo every March from 1988 until 1997.

As a "living historian," Edmondson has portrayed James Bowie, Sam Houston, and William Barret Travis for hundreds of classrooms and historical organizations. Edmondson also has portrayed Bowie for two History Channel documentaries, a Discovery Channel documentary, and an episode of Unsolved Mysteries.

# Credits

## Photo Credits

Cover: Texas State Preservation Board (Portrait); The Alamo © Lowell Georgia/CORBIS; p. 4 Texas State Preservation Board; p. 9 Hulton/Archive/Getty Images; p. 12 © 1999 Corbis; pp. 15, 23, 38, 44 Library of Congress Geography and Map Division Washington, D.C.; pp. 21, 81 Miriam and Ira D. Wallach Division of Art, Prints, and Photographs, the New York Public Library, Astor Lenox, and Tilden Foundations; p. 26 the Phelps Stokes Collection, Miriam and Ira D. Wallach Division of Art, Prints, and Photographs, the New York Public Library, Astor Lenox, and Tilden Foundations; p. 27 © Independence National Historical Park; p. 28 © CORBIS; pp. 30, 37, 68, 76, 96–97 Courtesy, Texas State Library and Archives Commision; p. 33 Library of Congress Prints and Photographs Division Washington, D.C.; p. 42 Texas General Land Office; pp. 46–47 Historic Arkansas Museum; p. 54 © Dave G. Houser/CORBIS; p. 57 Library of Congress, Prints and Photographs Division, Historic American Buildings Survey; p. 58 Historic American Buildings Survey (Library of Congress); p. 67 Tarlton Law Library, University of Texas School of Law; p. 70 Courtesy of the R.W. Norton Art Gallery, Shreveport, LA; p. 72 courtesy, Béxar County Spanish Archives; p. 74 © Bettmann/CORBIS; p. 85 David Crockett's Rifle, Gift of Mr. and Mrs. Paul L. Failor, The Alamo Collection, Photograph courtesy of the Daughters of the Republic of Texas Library; p. 86 Amon Carter Museum, Fort Worth; p. 89 DeGolyer Library, Southern Methodist University; p. 90 © National Portrait Gallery, Smithsonian Institution/Art Resource, NY.

## Editor

Joanne Randolph

## Series Design

Laura Murawski

## Layout Design

Corinne Jacob

## Photo Researcher

Jeffrey Wendt